D0548745
T2-COR-746

5⁰⁰

# The Stone Menagerie

by Shay Rieger

Charles Scribner's Sons
New York

# ACKNOWLEDGMENTS

The Shepherd Gallery, New York, N.Y.; Couturier Galerie, Stamford, Conn.; the private collections of R. H. Shepherd, Claire Nichtern, Joseph H. Hirshhorn; The New York Aquarium, Brooklyn, N.Y.; The Bronx Zoo, The Bronx, N.Y.; The American Museum of Natural History, New York, N.Y.

Special thanks to Emily Rieger, Bob Carrol, Maggie Brown.

Photographs by Eeva.

Page 18, middle, courtesy of The American Museum of Natural History.

Copyright © 1970 Shay Rieger / This book published simultaneously in the United States of America and in Canada / Copyright under the Berne Convention / All rights reserved / No part of this book may be reproduced in any form without the permission of Charles Scribner's Sons / Printed in the United States of America / Library of Congress Catalog Card Number 73-121748 / A-8.70[MZ]

*For Geo Bergal*

Stone comes from the earth and is heavy, but a sculptor can make it fly.

— Nick, age 11

Doing sculpture of animals in stone is like catching them and holding them forever.

— Alice, age 12

# INTRODUCTION

As a sculptor I have worked in many materials, such as clay, plaster, wood, and bronze, but I find carving in stone the most exciting. The very nature of the stone—its hardness and resistance—is a challenge to overcome with hammer and chisel. This challenge is met when a chunk of limestone or a block of marble is carved into a figure that is alive with form and feeling.

Each stone has a unique character and beauty. When choosing the right stone for my subject, I look at the colors and grainings as well as the texture, hardness, and shape. Sometimes a stone's shape determines the subject. A piece of limestone that I found in a city lot was already formed like a snail. I carved it just a little, set it on a base, and had a finished sculpture. Usually I pick a stone that bears no resemblance at all to my subject but that I feel will be striking or unusual. One example of this is a baby whale for which I chose a piece of pale pink alabaster.

Stones can be found everywhere. I have found them in the country, in city lots, and even in torn-down buildings. But most of the carving stones come from quarries. A quarry is a huge open hole in the earth where stones are dug out. They are cut into different sizes, then shipped to cities and to the artists' studios. I usually work with the size and weight I can handle, but when a stone is very heavy a pulley can be used for lifting and moving it.

When the stones become sculptures of fish, insects, and other animals, they are sent to the art gallery where they are placed on view. Because I believe that stone sculptures should be pleasant to the touch as well as to the eye, in my stone menagerie there is not one sign that says "Do not touch."

*Shay Rieger*

## CREATURES OF THE SEA

At the New York Aquarium in Brooklyn there are all kinds of fish, from a huge white whale to a tiny sea horse. The children are watching some of the big fish bob to the surface for air.

## The Whale

Down below, at the portholes of the tank, I can be at eye level with the fish. I can study them close-up as they glide, dive, or just swim along peacefully.

This white whale is fifteen feet long and weighs eighteen hundred pounds.

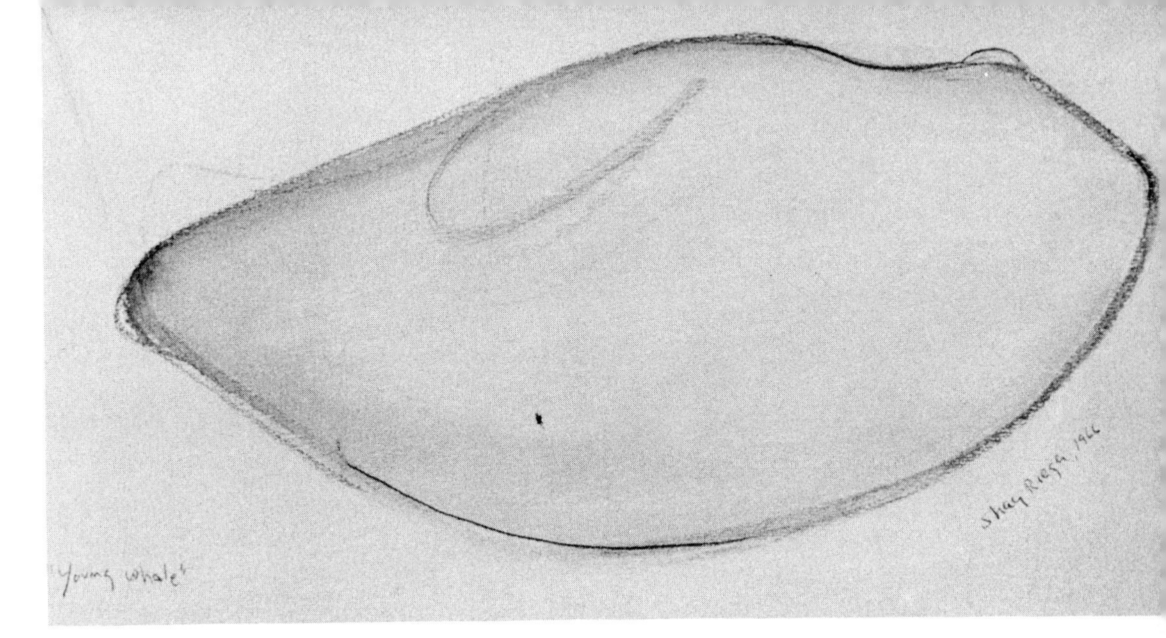


I make a quick drawing of a baby whale, sketching the fullness of the shape to remind me of his weight and volume when I do the carving. Since my aim is not just to make realistic animals but rather to capture a feeling or characteristic of the subject, I may simplify the form in my sketches or pick out features and exaggerate them.

I carved the baby whale in a pale pink alabaster. Using the right base for finished sculpture is very important. I chose this one with the metal pipe so that the alabaster whale seems to be floating.

## The Sea Horse

The sea horse is the only fish I ever saw that swims in an upright position.

This is my ink and watercolor sketch of the sea horse.

I carved the sculpture of the sea horse in white marble, polished smooth. This finish allowed me to emphasize the graceful S-curve of his body.

## The Stingray

Ray fish swim mostly in warm, tropical waters near the ocean floor. Because their bodies are flat they can hide in the sandy bottom of the sea. Some ray fish will inflict a brutal sting when attacked by other fish. Their sting can be dangerous to man, too.

The stingray looks to me like a swimming kite.

This is the finished sculpture of the ray. An impression of motion is created by the shape and angle of the wide fins and also by the dark red grainings within the alabaster stone.

## The Flying Fish

The flying fish, with its wing-like fins, swims swiftly to the surface, goes up into the air for a short distance, and plunges back into the water. In this way it escapes its enemies.

To emphasize its flying motion I exaggerate the wings in my drawing.

The wave-like design in this black and white alabaster adds to the feeling of movement in the sculpture of the flying fish.

## The Blowfish

This is my watercolor drawing of the blowfish, or puffer. When this fish is frightened it blows up like a balloon, and then it is not easy for other fish to swallow it.

The roundness of the alabaster and the circular patterns in the stone give the puffer its blown-up look.

When my sculptures are finished I send them to an art gallery. Here people of all ages come to see the work.

## The Penguin

Outside the aquarium is a lovely pond where these young penguins feel right at home.

While they are sunning and drying themselves I sketch them in these characteristic poses.

Here are my quick line drawings of the penguins. I plan to do a baby penguin and make him small and pudgy.

I used white marble, which I carved very rounded and squat, giving only a suggestion of the fins and webbed feet. I wanted to capture its simple form, its solidness and its closeness to the ground.

## LOOKING AND SKETCHING IN THE COUNTRY

I take a walk in the country to find some small animals to use as models. Under this rock I see a world of crawling creatures. And nearby, I am lucky enough to find a praying mantis.

The praying mantis is a large insect three to four inches long. He has three pairs of legs. The front pair often look like hands held in the position of prayer. Actually he uses his hands to catch and hold smaller insects.

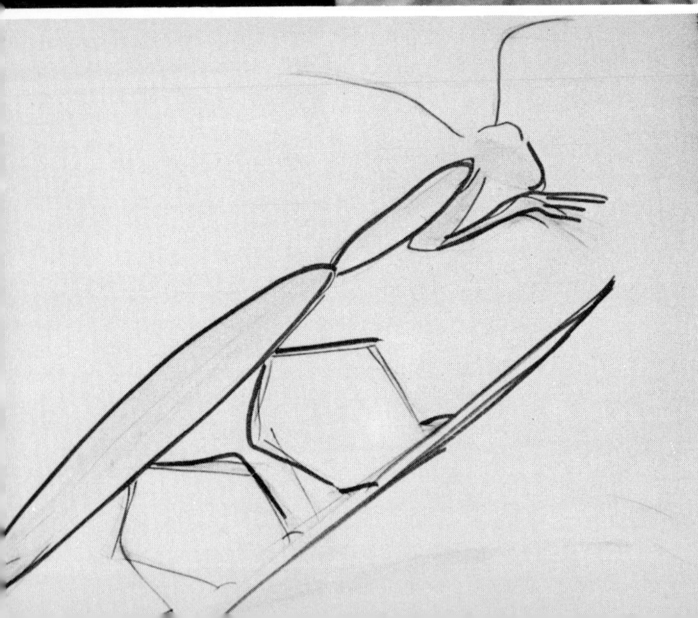

The one I found sat still just long enough for me to make some fast sketches before he disappeared in the grass.

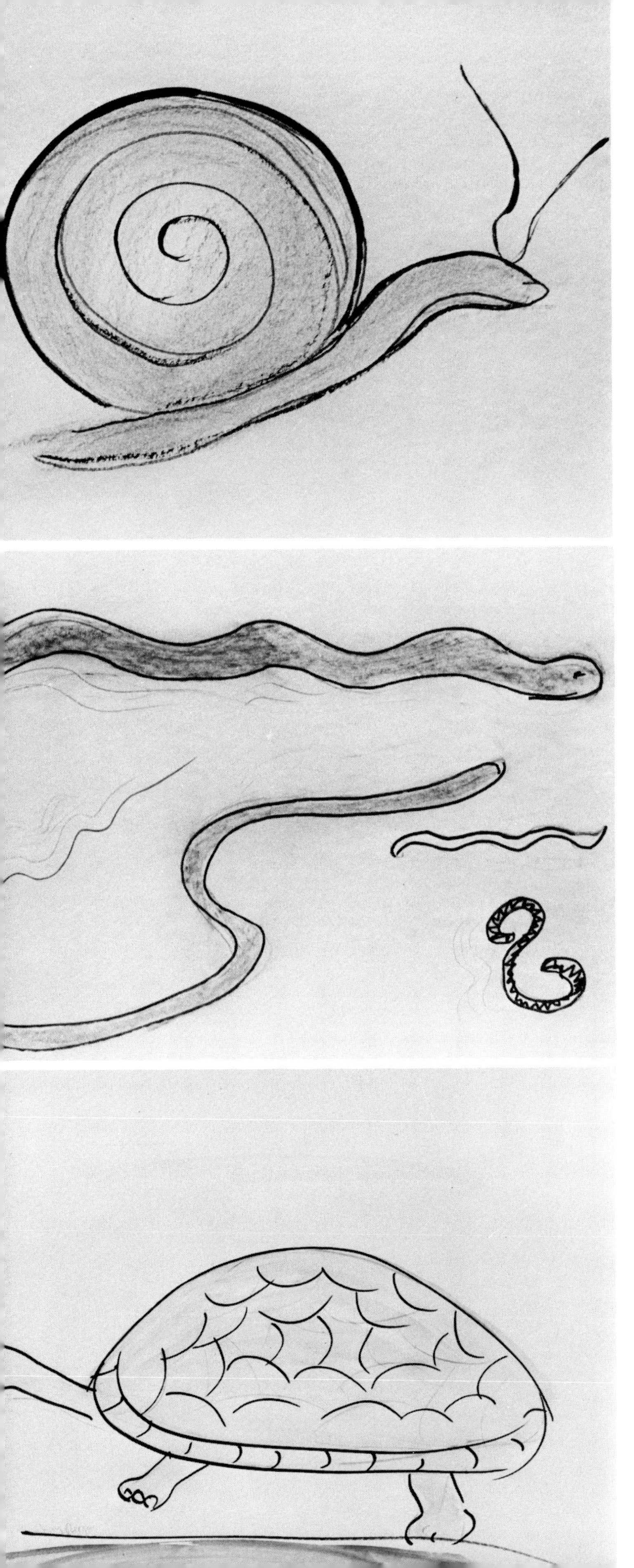

## The Snail

The land snail moves very slowly, maybe because he carries his house on his back.

## The Worms

These are sketches of the wiggly worms I saw under the rock.

## The Turtle

This turtle was taking a walk as I quickly sketched him.

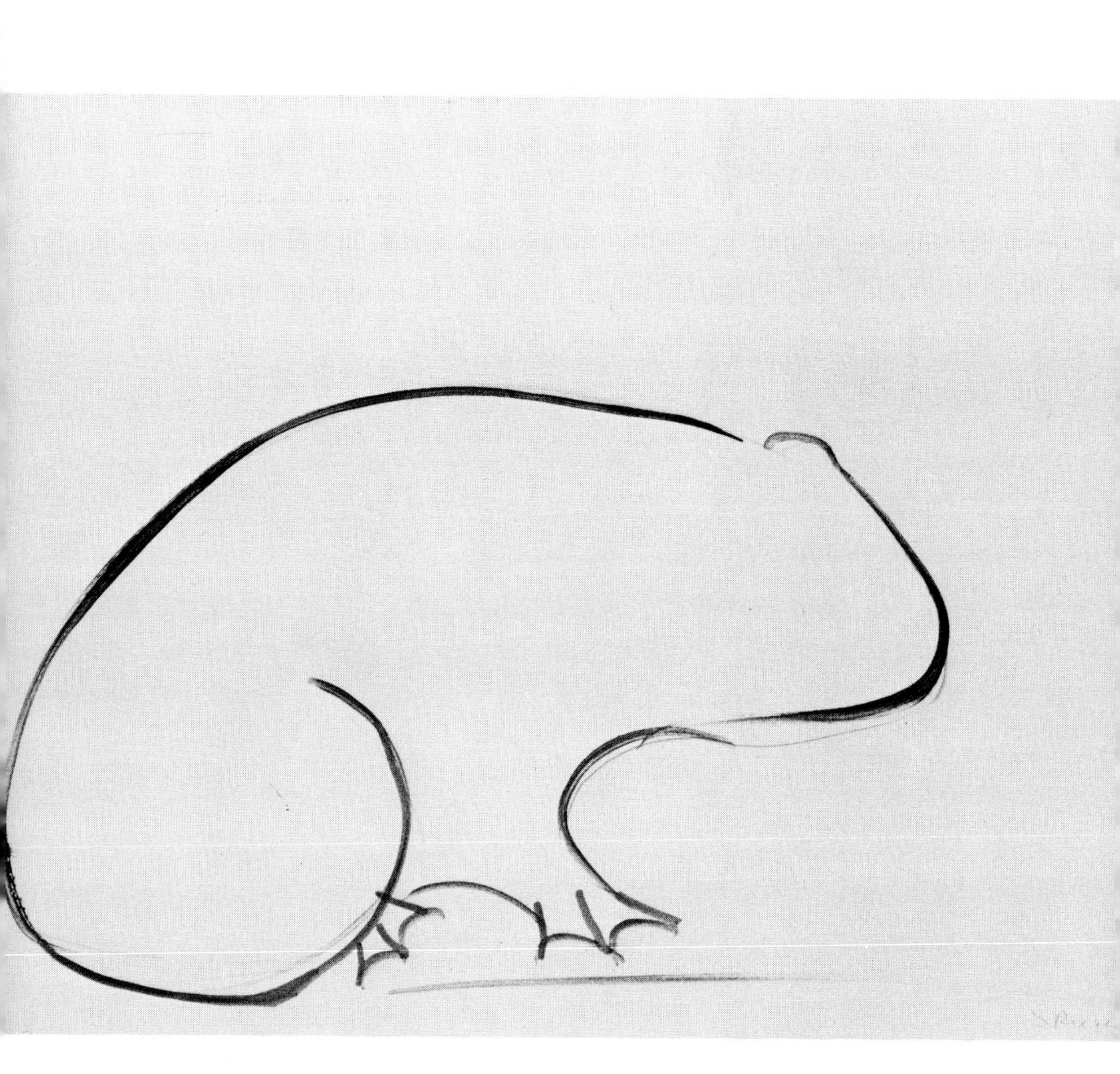

## The Frog

Often it is the simplest line that will capture the essence of a subject, as in this quick drawing of the frog.

The stones I use most often are marble, limestone, alabaster, and granite. By first wetting down a stone with water, I can see the colors and grainings and any defects, such as cracks or weak veinings.

## THE STONES TO CHOOSE FROM

Granite is the hardest of all stone. It originally comes from deep inside the earth where it is so hot that the granite is a liquid. Over millions of years it rises to the surface and cools and hardens. The colors of granite range from tints of pink to red and white and gray.

Limestone is a soft stone to carve. It is formed of the shells of sea animals and plants that died and settled to the ocean floor and after millions of years turned into limestone. I use mainly buff and white limestone, but there are also gray ones.

Marble was once limestone but was changed over a long period of time by natural forces, such as heat from deep under the sea and the weight of rocks and water bearing down on it. The beautiful colors of marble range from oranges, purples, and reds to snow white and jet black. Serpentine is a type of marble, green in color, which takes a high polish and can be made as smooth as glass.

Alabasters are softer and more delicate than most marble. They may be translucent or opaque. There are solid white alabasters and colorful ones mottled in active designs and patterns. The colors range from white, brown, and gold to delicate pinks with veinings of deep red.

Now I will describe from the beginning how I carve a sculpture. When I decide to do my carving of the praying mantis, I begin by looking at the sketches I made in the country. I recall his long, narrow body and bulgy eyes and the front legs that look like hands.

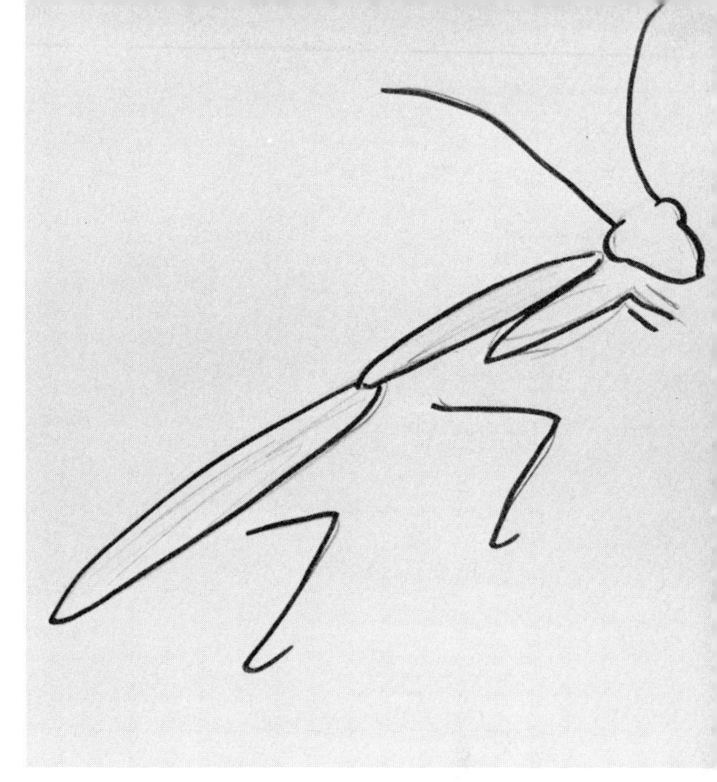

## A STONE FOR THE MANTIS

I choose a serpentine stone because the shape and the jade green color seem right for the insect. Also there is a subtle brown graining that hints of earth color, and this interests me, too.

## The Studio

At the studio everything is ready for work.

These are the tools used for carving the stones. Hammers and chisels do most of the chopping. The files and electric sander are for shaping and smoothing. A sculptor must always wear goggles for protection against the flying chips. The face mask is for protection from inhaling the stone dust.

With the hammer and chisel I begin to carve the stone. I hold the chisel in my left hand, which I aim or point at the section of the stone I want to chop away. In my right hand I hold the hammer and hit the top of the chisel.

The chips start flying.

## Carving the Mantis

I am chipping away freely to rough out the shape of the mantis. At this stage I pay little attention to detail.

After I have cut away much of the stone, it is as though I were freeing the mantis that lay hidden within the rock.

The body of the insect has become quite clear now. At the base I am making tool marks to separate it from the actual sculpture.

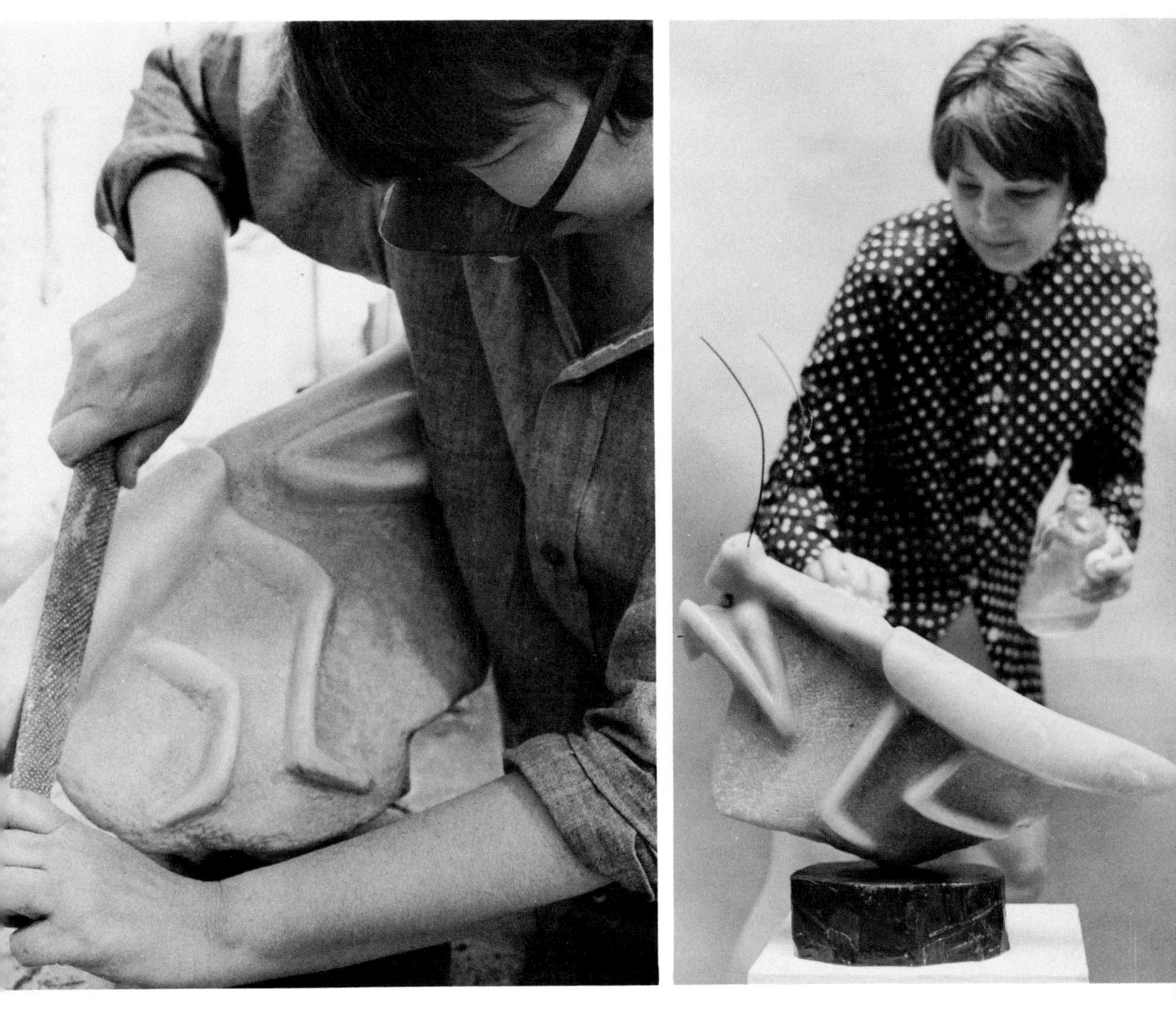

After much filing, rubbing, and sanding the stone takes on a high polish.

I have placed two wires in the mantis's head to represent his antennae, and now I wipe away the stone dust with some clear oil.

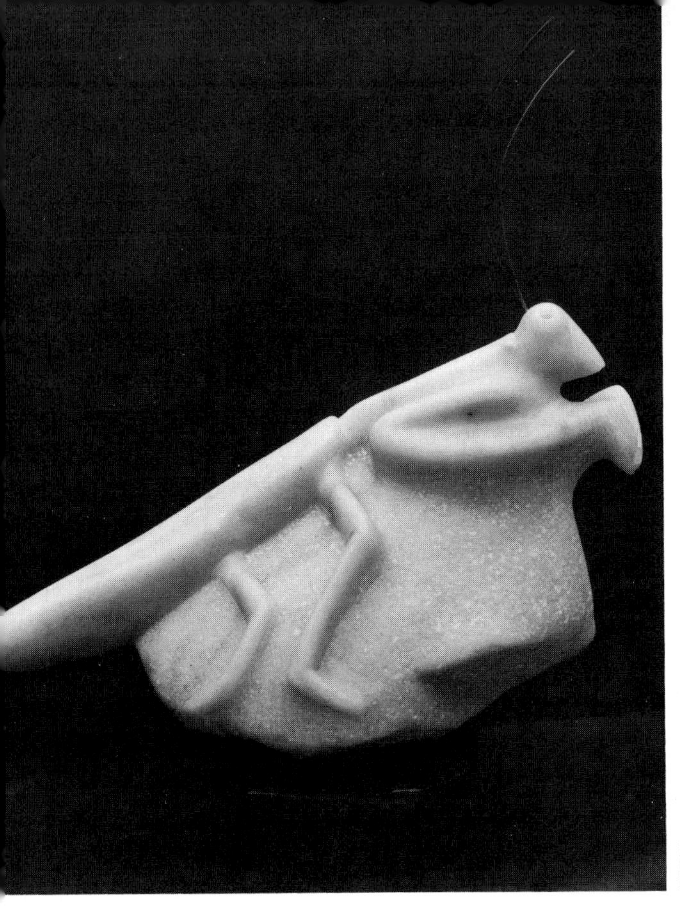

## The Mantis in the Gallery

After five weeks of work the praying mantis is finished. It is set on a rosewood base.

Then it is sent to the art gallery, where this little girl seems to think the mantis is real and tries to feed it.

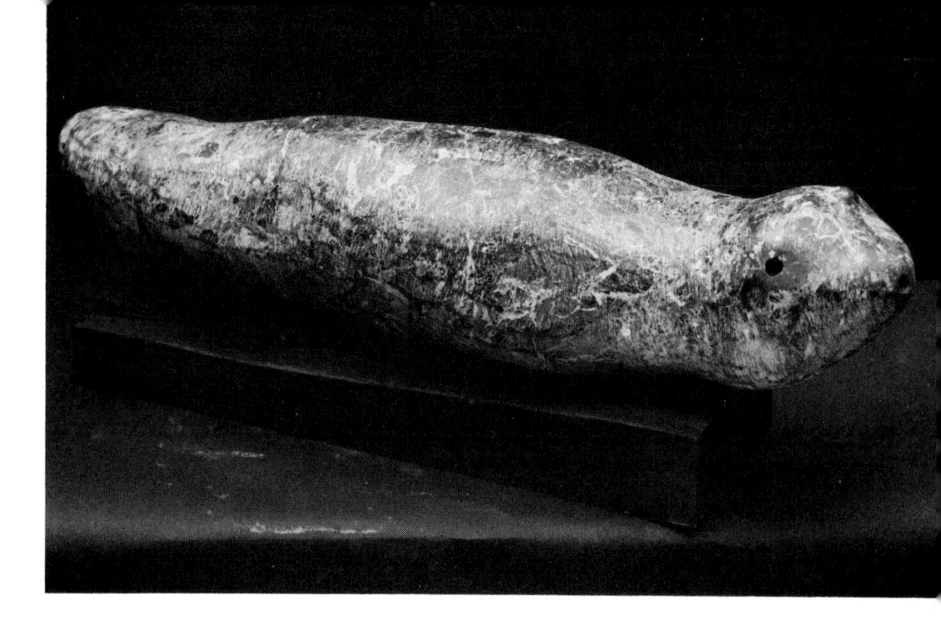

In the same way that I carved the mantis with the hammers and chisels, I also did the other animals, such as this sculpture of the worm. The stone I used for the worm is Italian marble actively mottled in red, purple, black, and white.

## THE OTHER COUNTRY ANIMALS

At the gallery this boy bends down to view the worm. Because the worm is an insect that crawls in the earth, the sculpture is set on a wooden base lower than the other animals in the gallery.

This is the limestone snail, left in the rough with the tool marks showing. The stone is a buff color, set on a dark slate base. This sculpture took very little carving because the piece of limestone looked so much like a snail already.

The turtle looks low and chunky in a grayish marble.

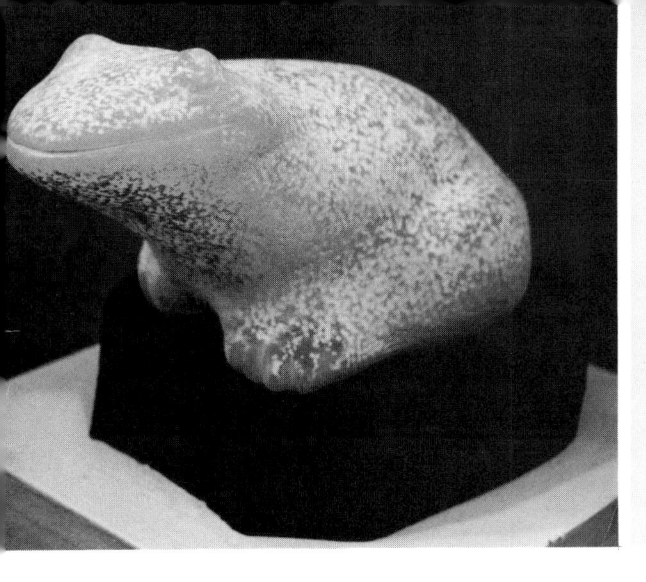

From the sketch of the frog that I did in the country I carved several sculptures, using different stones. In this white alabaster frog I left the tool marks showing to give some rough texture to the translucent stone.

This frog was done in granite with a lively pattern of reds, purples, and tints of yellow. Because granite is very hard and sometimes brittle, I do not use it often.

## The Frogs

This compact little frog is of cream-colored marble speckled with gold dots and polished smooth.

At the gallery the granite frog seems almost to be looking back at the little girl.

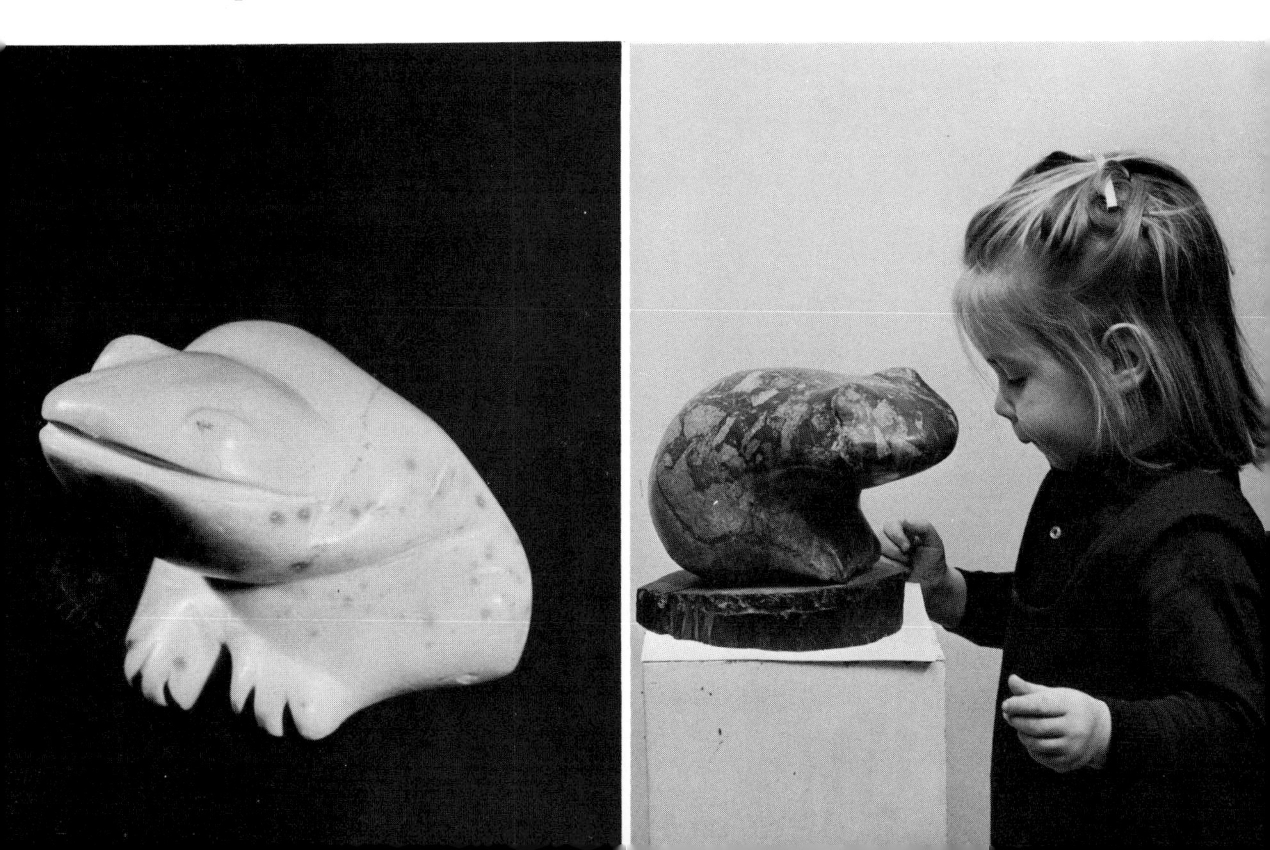

## SKETCHING AT THE MUSEUM

At the Museum of Natural History I am studying the anteater. This mounted specimen is of an anteater that is found in Africa.

Rather than copying the model exactly, I work into the drawing my ideas of how the anteater will look carved in stone. In this ink drawing I changed the curve of the tail, simplified the shape of the legs, and elongated the animal's body.

The finished sculpture was done in white marble. It was polished until it became very smooth. Two gold lines running across the body add a certain grace and length to the sculpture.

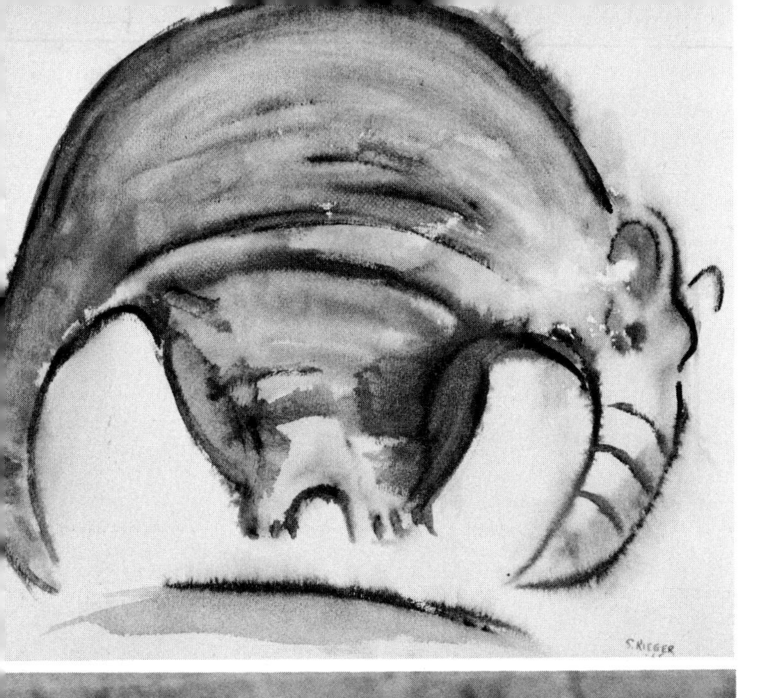

## The Anteater in the Gallery

This is a different impression of the same anteater, which I sketched in watercolor . . .

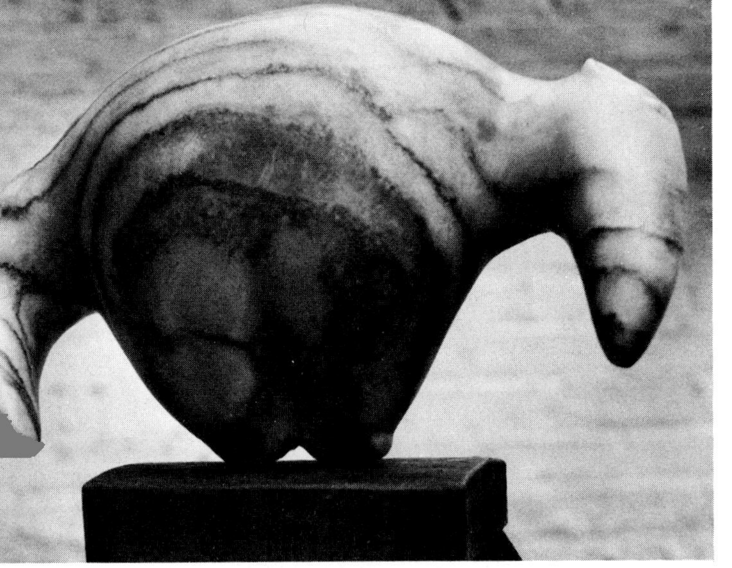

And the finished sculpture. The mottling in this alabaster blends in with the rhythm of the sculptural form.

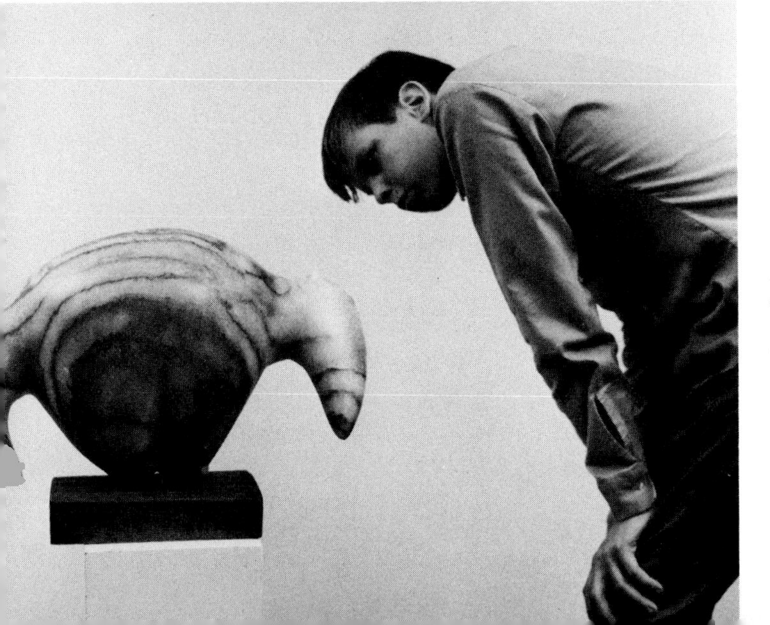

At the art gallery, a boy views the anteater from all sides.

## BIRDWATCHING AT THE ZOO

At the Bronx Zoo there is a large cage called the aviary, where many birds are kept. The cage is so large that the birds can fly freely around but they cannot fly away.

The aviary is filled with unusual and rare birds. As I look around for birds that I can recognize, I spot the familiar chickadee.

## The Chickadee

The chickadee is a solid-looking little bird with a confident, trusting air. A simple line drawing records his rounded shape and jutting tail.

This is my carving in pure white marble. I chose this stone to stress the compact form of the chickadee.

In the art gallery this little girl has come to see the chickadee. The marble worm is in the foreground.

## The Pelican

The pelican is a humorous-looking bird with a big pouch under his long bill for catching and storing fish. He has a heavy body, short legs, and webbed feet and when he walks he waddles from side to side.

My drawing of the pelican was done in ink and watercolor.

This block of limestone looked scarred and rough before it was carved into the pelican.

In the finished sculpture I simplified the pelican's features, making them all part of a single form. The tool marks soften the texture of the surface.

## The Puffin

Another name for the roly-poly puffin is “sea parrot” because of his parrot-like bill. He has short, rounded wings and a stubby tail.

In my watercolor drawing of the puffin I wanted to get down on paper its roundedness and some of its humorous quality.

I chose a piece of white Italian marble for the pudgy puffin. The tool-mark surface is similar to the pelican’s surface but in the marble the effect is more delicate.

These great horned owls stare back at me as I sketch them. They are also called hoot owls because of their deep-toned call of repeated "who-o-o-o's."

## The Great Horned Owl

A group of owls sketched in ink. There are more than a hundred species of owls in the world. Because of their compact sculptural shape and their enormous, haunting eyes they have always inspired artists as subjects for paintings and sculpture.

This is the finished sculpture of a great horned owl. It was done in limestone stained with oil paint and wax. Sometimes I will apply color to a stone to enliven the tone.

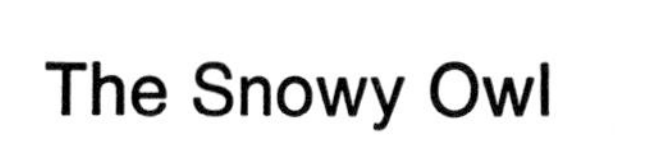

## The Snowy Owl

This young snowy owl is about to take his afternoon nap. Most owls do their hunting in the night. A full-grown snowy owl is a powerful bird and may grow as tall as two feet.

A quick sketch of the owl.

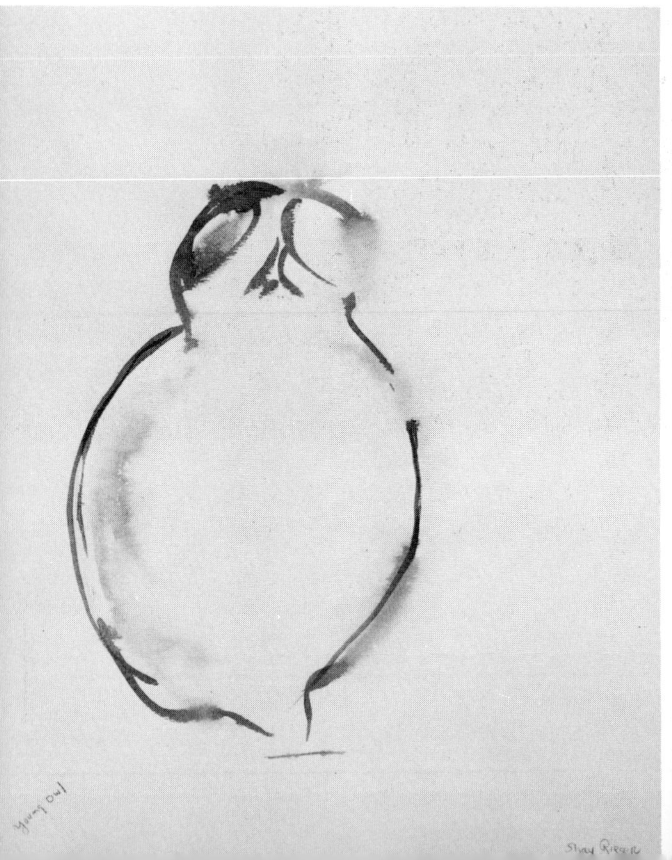


The snowy owl in white alabaster is perched on a log.

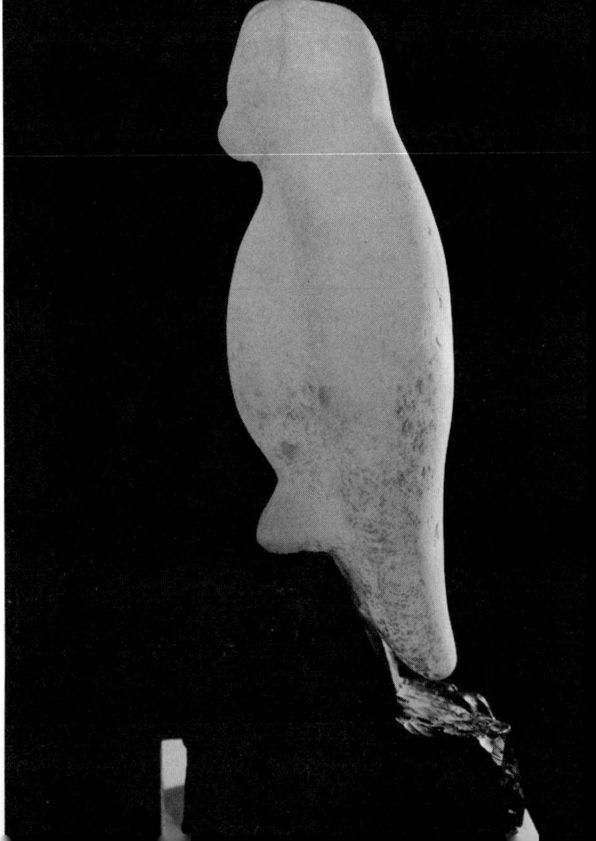

This lovely bird has a spoon-like shape at the tip of his bill. He sweeps his bill back and forth to catch and filter his food from the water. Some spoonbills nest low in the marshes while others nest in tall trees.

## The Spoonbill

I make a sketch of a young spoonbill.

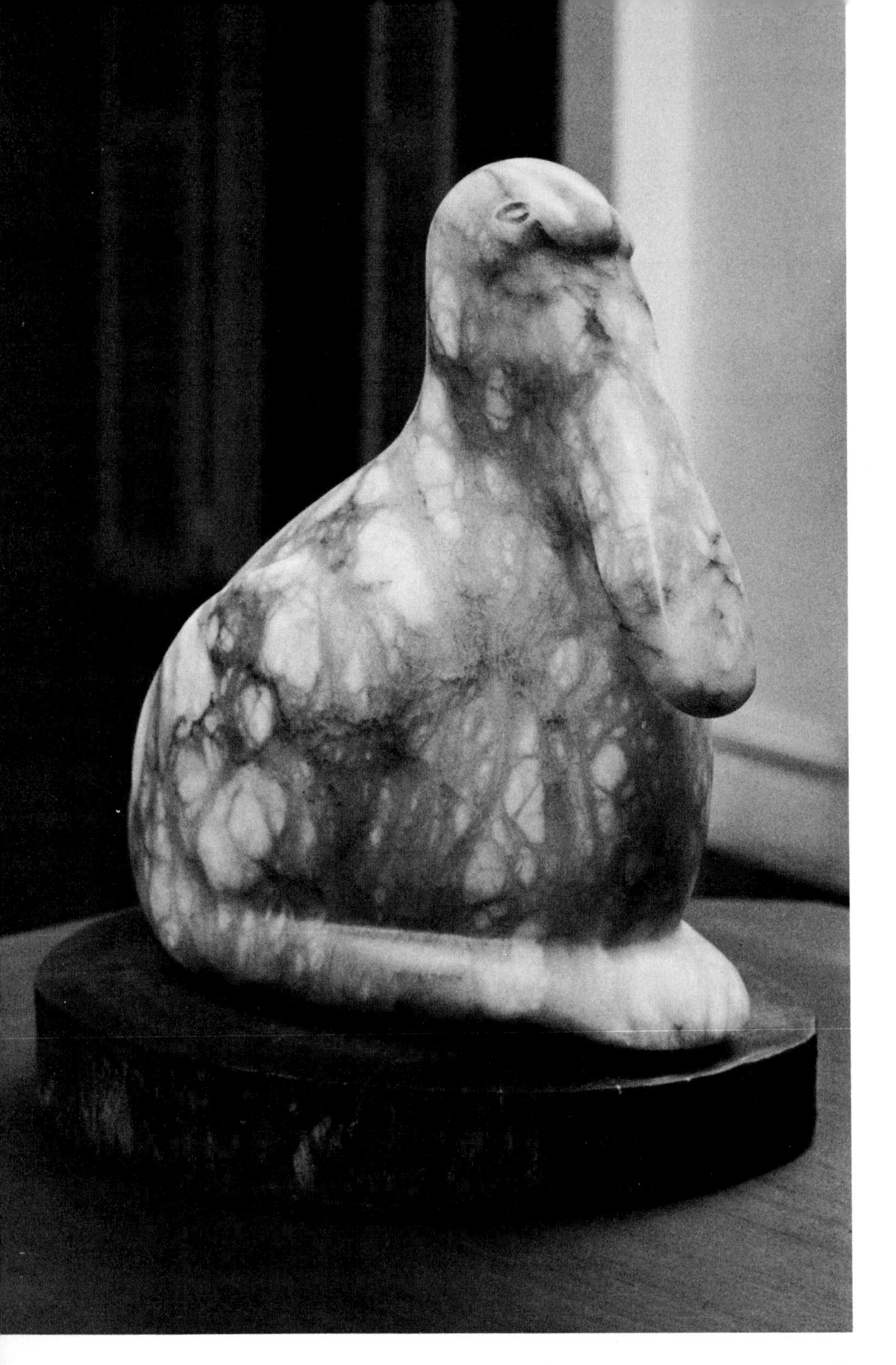

The finished sculpture of the young spoonbill looks very much like the drawing. The beautiful mottling in the black-and-white alabaster suggests a soft, feathery look, which was why I chose this stone for the spoonbill.

## The Spectacled Owl

Because of the white rims around their eyes, which look like glasses, these owls are called spectacled owls. They are brown and white and are found in Mexico and South America.

This is the spectacled owl that I carved in white limestone, finished in a rough texture.

In this sculpture there is an entirely different impression of the spectacled owl. The design within the alabaster resembles the lights and shadows of the forest where the owl lives.

## The Baby Owls

Baby owls are most appealing. I carved several in various stones, trying in each sculpture to convey their youth and innocent charm.

I did this one in serpentine marble, finely polished. It is like the stone I used for the praying mantis.

Another baby owl was carved in white alabaster. I have textured the surface with tool marks to contrast the body with the feet and beak, which are polished smooth.

## AT THE GALLERY

After two years, when all the sculptures are completed, they are exhibited in New York. Some people come to see what the artist intended to convey . . .

Others come not only to view the sculptures but to consider buying them . . .

And then there are those who bring to the work their own impressions and imagination . . .

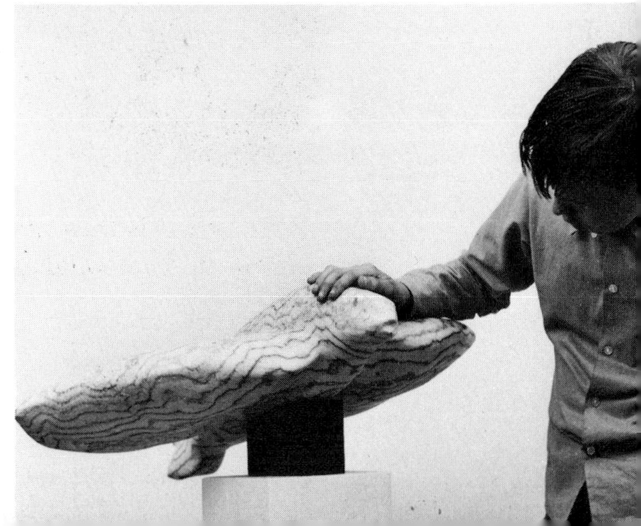

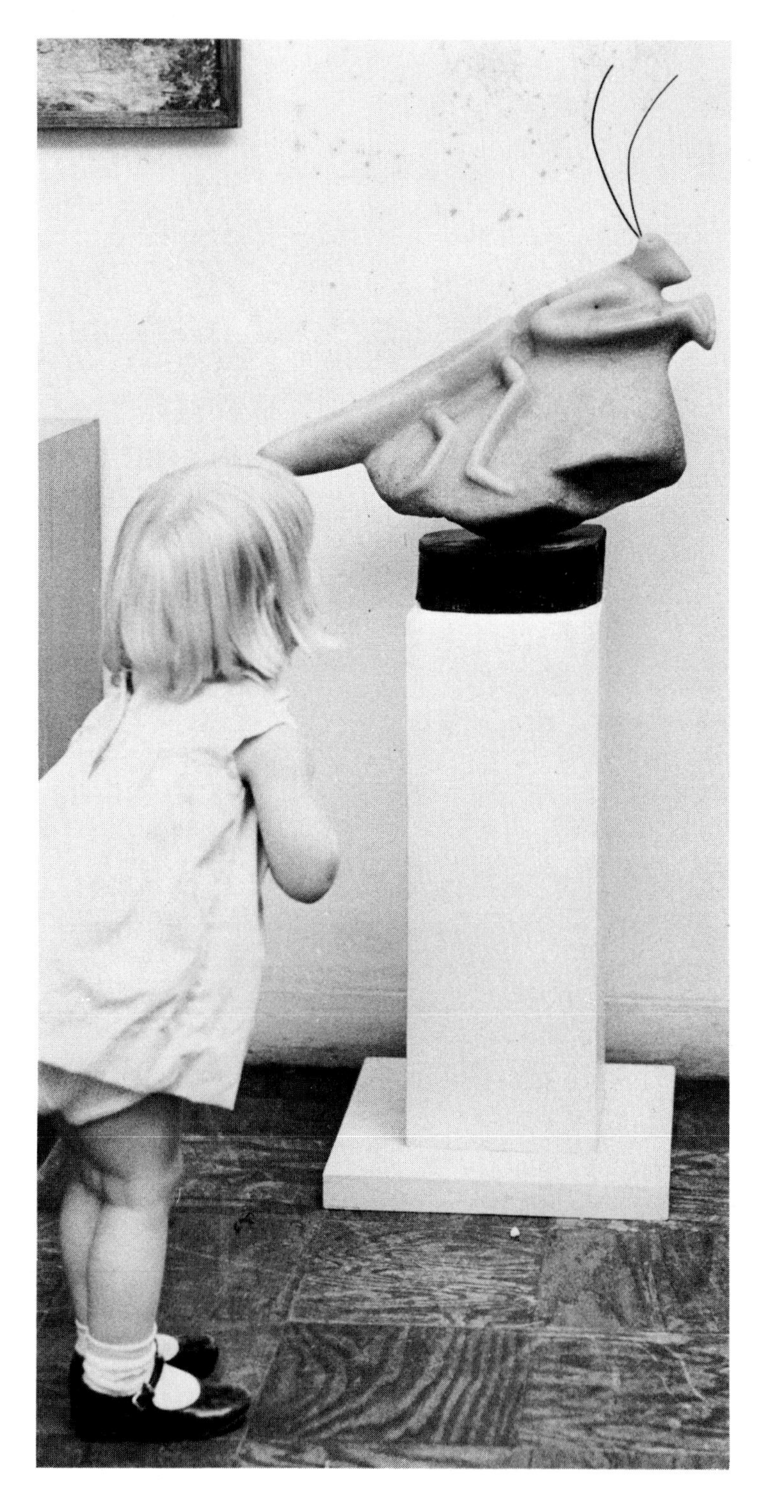

Whatever it is they may feel, looking at art is a very private and personal experience.